The Tree No One Wanted

The Tree
No One Wanted

A Modern Day Parable

GLENN H. GOREE

RESOURCE *Publications* · Eugene, Oregon

THE TREE NO ONE WANTED

Resource Publications
An Imprint of Wipf and Stock Publishers
199 W. 8th Ave., Suite 3
Eugene, OR 97401

www.wipfandstock.com

PAPERBACK ISBN: 978-1-5326-3737-7
HARDCOVER ISBN: 978-1-5326-3738-4
EBOOK ISBN: 978-1-5326-3739-1

Manufactured in the U.S.A.

I dedicate this book to my two awesome grandchildren, Xaia and Nico.

The Tree No One Wanted

There was once an enormous seed that seemed to appear out of nowhere. It was so large it looked like a displaced rock in the forest. The seed was hard, covered in pockmarks, and sported a dirty, brown outer shell. On the morning the odd-shaped seed materialized on the forest floor, it tried to wiggle its way deep into the soil. All the other newborn seeds were normal, small, and soft, with beautiful tan coloring, and resembled spear tips. Not only were they easier on the eye because they looked like seeds, but they were able to burrow into the soil more readily than the misshapen seed.

No matter how intensely the ungainly, rotund seed tried to tunnel itself deep into the life-giving earth, it could not burrow like the other seeds. One by one his fellow seeds found a home beneath the soil's surface and were quickly nourished by the nutrients and moisture they found. Meanwhile, Outsider, as the seed was nicknamed by the others, was only halfway buried and it seemed he could penetrate no deeper.

The rest of the seeds laughed at him and called him all sorts of degrading names because he was not handsome like they were. His plain and ugly exterior was reason enough for them to ignore him as they talked among themselves. Outsider epitomized the face that would look through a house's window from the street wishing he could join in the fun and games, but knew no one would notice him, let alone invite him in.

Finally, after what seemed an eternity, the large seed felt nutrients and moisture soaking into his thick coat even though he couldn't dig any deeper. Like all the other seeds, he began to submerge his roots deep into the soil to lay a foundation for a steady, secure new home.

As the forest of seeds grew, their slim, tender stems shot skyward, beautiful and as smooth as silk. That is, all except our huge, oddball seed. By all accounts, he should have produced a thick, strong stem. But no. His stem was as puny as a weed. It was less than half the height of the rest of the seedlings, bent and crinkled.

"What kind of tree are you going to be?" everyone asked.

All the other saplings and their parent trees took bets on whether or not he would survive the winter.

However, several years passed, and all the trees, except the tree no one wanted, had grown to become strong, tall, and study. Their parents were proud. In the dark of the evening, when no humans were around, the entire group of parent trees gossiped and bragged.

"My son will grow up one day to be a fine sturdy beam in a mighty house. He will hold the rest of the roof's weight and carry the load all by himself, for generations."

"That's nothing," another parent tree said. "My son will grow up to be the cross-beam over a mighty door in the governor's home. He will be so thick and solid those humans will abandon the use of the stone arch and use him alone."

"You two have nothing on *my* son. He will grow up so straight and tall he will be used as a mast on a Roman ship. He will tower above all other masts on the lead ship in the Roman Navy. He will travel the world and have tales to tell no one else around here has ever heard."

Finally, not to be out done, another mother and father tree spoke up and said, "Our son will be a mighty warrior. He will be made into the long beam of a catapult and will hurl massive stones thousands of feet to break down the walls of cities the Romans conquer."

Amidst all this chatter expressing ego, pride, and parental vanity, nothing was heard from the parents of the tree no one wanted. Seems they were the only two of their kind, and none of the other trees had seen where they came from either. As far at the forest inhabitants knew, this was the first time the odd trees had produced an offspring.

Like their seed, the odd parent trees had appeared in the forest unnoticed, grew to maturity, and lived in the shadows, keeping quietly to themselves. They were humble, and stood silently by, listening, not wanting to predict any future for their boy. They were content to let him be part of the forest, and grow to a nice old age, and die from natural causes. Several hundred years of life were reward enough. After all, he would provide shade for humans to en-joy. He could take care of the birds of the air and other forest creatures. And, if necessary, during floods or fires he could use his size to shield small saplings from being washed away or burned.

Many years later, the young trees, including our odd sapling, grew to maturity. No, he was not as big and handsome as the other trees, but he finally filled out and was content with the way he was made. He had already been helping humans and forest animals just like his parents predicted. Satisfied with his place, he felt no inner desire to become anything different. All the other trees continued to ridicule him by saying he had no ambition or desire to improve his lot in life.

Then, one spring day, a bevy of humans approached bearing axes and saws, and riding in large wagons. Now the time of reckoning had arrived. All the young, handsome trees wanted to shout, "Pick me! Pick me!" But they couldn't, so they had to wait and let their size do their talking.

Sure enough, each tree of the elite group was chosen, chopped down, and stacked in the wagons to be carted back to Jerusalem.

Just when the men were about to leave, one turned and stood in front of the tree no one wanted. Hands on his axe, he said, "What a strange looking tree. Let's cut it down anyway."

The men completed the task and added the tree no one wanted to the last wagon-load. The other trees already in the wagon were indignant. They said amongst themselves, "How dare these humans mix us with that useless stick?"

However, since they couldn't inform the humans of their social blunder, the trees remained silent. The tree no one wanted didn't care about what they said. He was sad because he would not live out his life in the forest. But he had an inkling that being cut down and moved to Jerusalem would provide an adventure he hadn't anticipated.

When the wagons arrived in the bustling city of Jerusalem, the lumbermen displayed the wood for discerning carpenters.

One said, "I'll take this tree to became a crossbeam in a mighty house."

"And I want this one for the beam over a door in the ruler's home," said the second carpenter.

"This extra tall tree will become a mighty mast on a ship I'm building for the Roman Navy." The proud builder pounded his chest.

Not to be outdone, the last carpenter stood next to a fine-looking tree and said, "I have plans for this specimen. It will be perfect for the long beam of a catapult."

As the parent trees predicted, each of their handsome offspring became the wooden fixtures in the human world they had wanted.

What about the tree no one wanted? Ridicule was added to insult. It wasn't enough for each tree to be taken for a magnificent human endeavor, but they each jeered and cursed the tree no one wanted as they left.

"Hey, sap," said one. "That's all you're good for."

"Why don't you turn over a new leaf? Oh, that's right, now that you've been cut down you can't grow any new leaves."

"Hey my man, I think you're barking up the wrong tree. You're nothing like us. You're not in the same class."

But the tree no one wanted ignored their hurtful remarks and was content to be left in the carpenter's storage area where the man stowed fresh-cut wood from the forest. After all, what else could the tree do?

It seemed no human had any grand or noble tasks in store for him. In fact, one day he heard a few carpenters questioning why the logger had bothered to cut down the tree.

Many months later, the humans still had no use for the tree no one wanted.

Used to criticism and ugly words, he still cringed every time a carpenter entered the storage area. The morning one mentioned using the tree for firewood was the worst day of his life.

After thinking about his eventual end, he saw a brief silver lining and accepted that even if he was turned into firewood, at least his flames would keep humans warm and cook their food. He would still be serving humans, and he was pleased.

Then one day, lo and behold, the tree no one wanted was selected and taken to a carpenter's shop. He was cut into two thick beams, one shorter than the other. A soldier in uniform collected the shorter beam, splintery and roughly cut, and took it to a place where a man was being whipped.

The tree no one wanted could hardly believe his eyes. Only man used barbed whips to tear away his fellow man's bark right down to the inner rings. So cruel. When the beam noticed all the red sap pouring from the man's back, he was sure the victim was going to die.

Then Roman soldiers angrily grabbed the man from the pool of his red sap spreading on the stone portico, and in the next instant, heaved the beam of the tree no one wanted across the doomed man's shoulders. His red sap soaked into the tree's wood fibers. Dismay showered over the tree no one wanted as his position forced him to rub against the convicted man's flesh. The beam wailed when soldiers whipped the man over and over. While lashing the convicted man, the Romans commanded him to walk. But how could he? After all, his roots, or what humans called legs, were cut and bleeding. And his branches, what humans called arms, were also covered in oozing slash marks. Guilt overwhelmed the tree no one wanted. How could he justify being carried by a human so near death?

The tree no one wanted decided to break an ancient law that harked back to creation, to the brotherhood of trees. He resolved to speak on behalf of the condemned man. After all, with the crowd's shouting and cursing, and a few resolute men demanding the man's release, the tree's voice would not be distinguishable. So shout he did as loud as he could, and although his words of condemnation did indeed blend in with the human crowd, they had no influence over the soldiers.

Midst the commotion, the beam pondered the situation again. Why did so many people hate this man? Why did so few ask for his release? What could this human have done to generate so much violence and evil?

In order for trees to survive from season to season, they have to be sensitive to the world around them. Hence, the tree no one wanted could feel in his rings, all the way to his core that this mob encompassed more than civil unrest. He hated the fact he was forced to be an unwilling participant in the violence, but he realized there was more at stake than this human's untimely death.

Suddenly, a power larger than nature overwhelmed him, filling him with the knowledge that he had a part to play in this human's life. Although he didn't want to admit it, his fate was sealed by a destiny beyond this world.

Wincing, the shorter beam from the tree no one wanted bobbed up and down on the convicted man's shoulders as he staggered through the streets dragging one foot after the other. The beam looked backward and saw a trail of the human's red sap. How could people be so hideously malicious? Many spat on the man, while some hurled rocks and rotten vegetables. Trees would never do this their kith and kin.

On and on they slogged through the riotous crowd. The beam held back his tears and tried to make himself lighter. How he wished he could relieve the man of his burden completely. He strained to see over the mob. Where were the soldiers taking this convicted human being?

In the meantime, the longer beam of the tree no one wanted had been hauled to the top of a hill that looked like a skull. He watched as Roman soldiers dug a hole and then spread out two sections of rope and four iron nails. The nails were rusty, dirty, and oh, so thick. What were the men doing exactly? The longer beam shrugged. Maybe he'd discover their intent soon. Even though the beam lay on the ground near the hole, he'd been placed at just the right angle on the hill so he could see an angry crowd of humans climbing up the trail.

Squinting, he studied the mob. Was that the other half of himself across the red-sap covered shoulders of a human? By the sneering and jeering sounds, the longer beam determined the man to be a criminal. What part was his other half to play in the condemned man's future?

Just then, the crowd parted. The convicted man could barely stand. Head bowed, his knees buckled, and he fell to the rocky ground. The longer beam flinched as his other half fell, too.

The full weight of the shorter beam of the tree no one wanted crashed down on the man's back and shoulders. The beam wanted to sob but the crowd had diminished and he dare not utter a word.

"What's happening now?" the shorter beam silently asked as soldiers aligned him on the ground.

He didn't have long to wait. The soldiers dragged the convicted man to the beam and shoved him down. Centered on the beam with his arms outstretched, the man did not struggle. Not one bit, not even as nails were pounded through his wrists. The shorter beam of the tree no one wanted recoiled with each pounding of the hammer that drove the nails into both ends of his wooden body.

The convicted man yelled in agony, but not as much as the beam expected. In his youth, he'd heard men scream louder when they accidentally scraped themselves against an axe. During their trek through the town and up the hill, the man had tolerated the abuse with a stoicism the beam had never encountered in a human before.

With the convicted man secured to the shorter beam, the soldiers hoisted their burden onto the longer beam and lashed the two together. Once again, the two beams became one. They shared their separate experiences in a blink of an eye. The beams of the tree no one wanted wailed silently as the convicted man screamed while his feet were nailed onto the longer beam. Soldiers then used ropes to hoist up the tree no one wanted, dragged it to the previously dug hole, and stacked rocks at the base to stabilize it.

The tree no one wanted glanced to the left and to the right. By the mob's comments, he knew the men, one on each side on similar beams, were thieves. Many hours passed while the crowd waited for the convicted men to die.

Finally, when the three men were pronounced dead, their bodies were removed from the crosses which were then torn down and piled together to be burned at a later time.

When all the humans were gone, the three crosses felt safe to talk. They all lamented over being used for the taking of human lives. In the midst of their sorrow, a dove flew down and landed on the pile of beams.

She announced, "I have been sent from God who has known you all from the time you were seeds."

"Truly?" asked one cross as the tears of all the trees fell to the ground still soaked with the red sap from the humans.

"I want to know why we were used for such evil?" another cross asked.

"Why have you come to us now?" asked the cross made from the tree no one wanted.

The Dove flapped her wings. "You three were chosen from birth to be here this day. You all came from the same type of tree, unique for what God planned. You may ask what type of tree was used to make the cross that crucified His Son, but no one will ever know the truth. Why? Because there will never be another tree like you again."

"I can understand that," said the tree no one wanted. His sobs began to subside so he could catch his breath and talk more clearly.

"Not me," said another tree. "I wanted to be like all the other trees in the forest."

The third tree poked through the pile. "Hush. Let's hear what the Dove has to say."

"Your births were unusual and your lives were different. God knew the other trees where you lived would make fun of you. It was all part of His plan. You were deliberately created to be uniquely common. God wanted all three of you to be plain and ordinary, almost ugly. You were each chosen for this special purpose."

The trees settled down to hear more from God's messenger.

"One of you was chosen for the thief who defended the Savior, while another was chosen for the thief who cursed and ridiculed the Savior. And finally, the third tree was chosen to be the cross on which the Savior of mankind would die."

No sooner had the Dove expressed these words than the tree no one wanted shouted out, "That was me, wasn't it!"

"Yes." The Dove bowed her head.

"I knew it. As soon as I was placed across the Savior's shoulders, I sensed a divine presence, but at the time I didn't know how to explain it. All day long I was overwhelmed with the knowledge that becoming a cross for a condemned man was only a small act. Now I understand. He was not just any man. He was the Savior of mankind."

The Dove swept her wing over the tree no one wanted. "You're right. That's why, of the three trees, you were the plainest and the most mocked and scorned in life to prepare you for this day. This is a happy day! A joyous day! It's a day of celebration!"

The tree who no one wanted asked, "How can this be? My human died."

The other two crosses echoed the same sentiment.

Raising her head, the Dove replied, "You are all correct. Your humans died." She pointed to the tree no one wanted. "But your human will rise in three days to conquer death. As the Creator's Son, He came from heaven to die as a sacrifice for man's sins, a sacrifice only He could make."

One of the other trees asked, "What part did my human play?"

"Will my human also rise from the grave?" asked the third tree.

The Dove swayed back and forth as if choosing just the right words. "One of the humans accepted the Savior as his Lord and King, while the other rejected Him. I'm sorry to be the one to deliver the news, but this is the way it will be until the end of time. Humans will either accept the Savior or reject Him. It's up to each human to make a choice. Didn't you notice this phenomenon among the people at the crucifixion? There were many who received Him as Savior, but there were even more who rejected Him. As it was today, so it will be until the end of time."

Then the tree who no one wanted stated, "But I feel so guilty! I was used to kill my human. This is against our tree law."

Nodding, the Dove replied, "I understand your reaction. But remember, you were made common so that you would be viewed by other trees as plain and unpretentious. In the same way, the Savior came from a humble family and lived a simple life. God chooses the meek and ordinary to show His strength.

The tree no one wanted bowed his head and sighed. "That's humbling."

In preparation for leaving, the Dove hopped to the highest beam which was part of the tree no one wanted. "From this day forward until the end of time, you will achieve fame. The symbol of the Cross will become the symbol of the Savior's faith. The Crucifix will provide hope, peace, and comfort to those who seek solace. You won't be remembered as the tree on which the Savior died. You will be celebrated as the Cross that made it possible, through the death of the Son of God, for mankind to have eternal life." She then fluttered her wings, soared into the heavens, and disappeared.

During the night, Roman soldiers trudged up the hill and set fire to the wood that formed the three crosses. Did they know the historical significance of what they were doing?

Quietly, the three trees burned, not completely without company. The Spirit of God hovered over the fire as the cracking embers disintegrated into ashes. If human eyes witnessed what happened next, they may report that the ashes were carried away by the wind. But they'd be in error. The ashes from the three crosses were wafted through the air by the Holy Spirit, spread throughout the earth to broadcast the Good News to all of nature that the tree no one wanted brought salvation to humanity through his obedience to God's plan.